Nature Explorers

Big Cats

by Annabelle Lynch

WINDMILL BOOKS

New York

Published in 2016 by **Windmill Books,**
an Imprint of Rosen Publishing
29 East 21st Street, New York, NY 10010

Series editor: Julia Bird
Series consultant: Catherine Glavina
Series designer: Peter Scoulding

Photo Credits: Guido Bissattini/Shutterstock: 18-19, 22tr. Volodymyr
Burdiak/Shutterstock: front cover, 12-13, 22cl. Dennis W Donohue/
Shutterstock: 6. Ehtesham/Shutterstock: 1, 5tl. enciktat/Shutterstock:
10-11, 22cr. Isselee/Dreamstime: 5bl. Eric Isselee/Shutterstock: 5tr. Ryan
Ladbrook/Shutterstock: 5br. Maggie Meyer/Shutterstock: 8-9. Petar
Paunchev/Shutterstock: 21, 22bl. Stuart G Porter/Shutterstock: 14-15, 22tl.
Stayer/Shutterstock: 4, 22br. Julian W/Shutterstock: 16-17.

Cataloging-in-Publication Data

Lynch, Annabelle.
Big cats / by Annabelle Lynch.
p. cm. — (Nature explorers)
Includes index.
ISBN 978-1-5081-9053-0 (pbk.)
ISBN 978-1-5081-9054-7 (6-pack)
ISBN 978-1-5081-9055-4 (library binding)
1. Felidae — Juvenile literature. 2. Cat family (Mammals)
I. Lynch, Annabelle. II. Title.
QL737.C23 L96 2016
599.75—d23

Manufactured in the United States of America

CPSIA Compliance Information: Batch #BW16PK: For Further Information
contact Rosen Publishing, New York, New York at 1-800-237-9932

Contents

Roar!

Lions, tigers, leopards, snow leopards, and jaguars are big cats. They can all roar.

Snow leopard

Tiger

Leopard

Lion

Black jaguar

Homes

Big cats live
in grasslands,
forests, or snowy
mountains.

What big
cats eat

All big cats eat meat. They catch other animals to eat.

Teeth

Big cats have sharp teeth to catch and eat animals.

Fur

Big cats have thick fur. The fur can have spots or stripes.

13

Big cat babies

Big cats have
babies called cubs.

Playing

Big cats love to play!
They chase each other
and play at fighting.

Rest

After playing, big cats need lots of sleep.

ZZZZZZzz

Pet
cats

Pet cats are from the same family as big cats. Do you have a pet cat?

Word bank

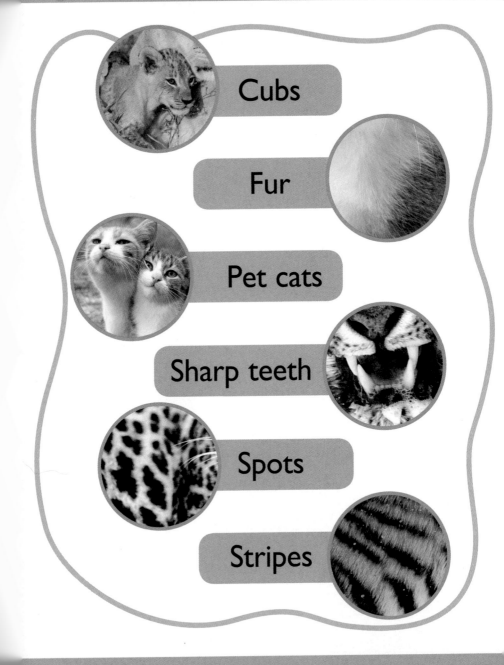

Cubs

Fur

Pet cats

Sharp teeth

Spots

Stripes

Quiz

1. Big cats can all

a) shout
b) roar
c) talk

2. Big cats eat

a) grass
b) apples and oranges
c) meat

3. Big cats have babies called

a) chicks
b) cubs
c) pups

Turn over for answers!

Nature Explorers are structured to provide support for newly independent readers. The books may also be used by adults for sharing with young children.

Starting to read alone can be daunting. **Nature Explorers** help by providing visual support and repeating words and phrases. These books will both develop confidence and encourage reading and rereading for pleasure.

If you are reading this book with a child, here are a few suggestions:

1. Make reading fun! Choose a time to read when you and the child are relaxed and have time to share the book.

2. Talk about the content of the book before you start reading. Look at the front cover. What expectations are raised about the content? Why might the child enjoy it? What connections can the child make with their own experience of the world?

3. If a word is phonically decodable, encourage the child to use a "phonics first" approach to tackling new words by sounding the words out.

4. Invite the child to talk about the content after reading, returning to favorite pages and pictures. Extend vocabulary by examining the Word Bank and by discussing new concepts.

5. Give praise! Remember that small mistakes need not always be corrected.

Answers

Here are the answers:

1. b   2. c   3. b

Index